The Eagle Flew

by Daniel Stokes
illustrated by Aisha Lani Wiig

ALKION PRESS

To Claire who has always gently nudged me forward. — DS

To my parents who encouraged me to swim upstream and follow my heart. — ALW

Copyright © 2022 Daniel Stokes and Aisha Lani Wiig
All rights reserved. No part of this book may be reproduced
in any form without written permission by the publisher
Layout: Ella Manor Lapointe
First published in 2022 by Alkion Press
14 Old Wagon Road, Ghent, NY, 12075
Alkion-Press.com
ISBN 978-1-7366829-7-5
Printed with the support of the Alkion Press Fund

The Eagle Flew

by Daniel Stokes
illustrated by Aisha Lani Wiig

High upon a cliff stood a large Oak Tree. His roots were firmly anchored in the rocky cliff so that when Brother Wind blew, the Oak Tree was steady and strong. He loved to watch Mother and Father Eagle flying high above him and it gave him great happiness when they chose to build their nest in his branches.

One morning the Oak Tree awoke to the sound of squawking and crying. He looked into the eagles' nest and what did he see? The four eggs that Mother and Father Eagle had so patiently cared for were cracked apart. Four scrawny, crying, hungry little baby eaglets lay nestled together. His branches creaked with joy.

All that day Father and Mother Eagle flew back and forth bringing food to their hungry little ones. The Oak Tree made sure he had a firm grip in the rocky cliff and that Brother Wind would not blow too hard. He also kept a sharp lookout for the dragon lizards that lived near the river in the valley below. They were known to climb the high cliffs and into the trees to eat young birds.

The clear summer days passed, and with the patient care of Mother and Father Eagle, the four little eaglets began to grow soft, brown, downy feathers.

One day they were watching their mother and father flying high above the valley.

"I'm going to fly just like that," said the first little eaglet.

"My wings will be the fastest," said the second.

"My wings will be the strongest," said the third.

But the fourth little eaglet said nothing.

"Look down at the river," said the first little eaglet.
They all looked down over the nest.
"I see some fishermen casting their nets," said the second eaglet.
"I can't wait to fly down there and catch a fish for mother and father," said the third little eaglet.
But the fourth little eaglet said nothing. It was a long way to the bottom of the valley.

As they sat and watched they saw a Dragon Lizard sunning himself on the rocks below. "When I get big, I'm going to thrash that Dragon Lizard,"
said the first little eaglet.
"He'll never catch me," said the second.
"I'll make him sorry he ever ate a bird," said the third.

But the fourth little eaglet said nothing.

One morning, Mother and Father Eagle came to the nest and said, "Now, my younglings, it is time for you to learn to fly. You've grown too big for the nest. Do not worry. When you spread your wings, Brother Wind will carry you aloft and you will feel the freedom of the sky.
Only take care not to go down to the river, for young wings can become tired and the dragon lizards know this. Now, who will go first?"

"I will, mother. I will soar with Brother Wind," said the first little eaglet, and he climbed up onto the edge of the nest. "Spread your wings, my dear," said Mother Eagle. She nudged the little eaglet with her beak. They all held their breath as he dropped down over the edge.

Suddenly, Brother Wind caught him, lifting him high across the valley. He soared back and forth, his eyes sparkling in the sun.

"I will go next, Mother," said the second little eaglet. "I will soar with Brother Wind."
She too, climbed to the edge of the nest, and in a flash, she was gone, flying with her brother high in the blue sky.

"I will go next, Mother," said the third little eaglet. "I will soar with Brother Wind." Soon, he too, had leapt over the edge, and now three young eaglets were winging their way, high among the clouds.

Mother Eagle turned to her fourth little one who was sitting quietly with wide, frightened eyes. Mother Eagle understood and said, "Perhaps you will be ready tomorrow."

Every day the fourth little eaglet watched her brothers and sister laughing and swooping across the sky. She wanted to fly more than anything but her feathers froze with fear when she looked over the edge. Each day, Mother Eagle asked, "And now, my youngling, are you ready to spread your wings and fly with Brother Wind?"

"I'm not ready yet, mother," she would reply.

One day she was huddled alone in the nest while her mother and father had flown far down the valley in search for food. Her bold brothers and sister were flying high above the river valley far out of sight.

Suddenly, she heard a faint cry that came from the river below. A moment later, she heard it again, this time, shriller and sharper. She certainly had the eyes of an eagle, for far below she saw her brother flapping his wings and crying for help. He was caught in a fisherman's net. The more he flapped his wings, the more entangled he became. He looked like he would drown.

The little eaglet knew that only she could help, but was there time?
Then she heard a low, rumbling voice.
"You must fly little eaglet; only you can save him."
It was the voice of the Oak Tree.

With courage she did not know she had, she leapt from the edge of the nest, diving down, down, down. Brother Wind saw her flight and swept her along on his magic carpet of air. So swiftly she flew. Her wings were like fire as she swooped down. In an instant she was untangling her brother from the net with her strong beak.

At last, she freed her brother from the net but his drenched wings were too tired and heavy to fly. With her strong talons she lifted him out of the water.

With all her strength she carried
her brother, up, up, up, the face of the rocky cliff.
Higher and higher she flew.
Above them, the Oak Tree swayed his branches, urging
her to fly ever higher and to hold on tight. Slow, but
determined, she rose up in the air until, at last, she pulled
her brother into the safety of the nest.
The Oak Tree thought he would burst with pride.

That evening the whole family gathered round her and stroked her strong feathered wings. She felt so brave now and she knew that, just like the Oak Tree, she too had a voice inside of her; a voice that she would always trust.

When her family was asleep,
she flew up to the highest
branch of the tree. As the full moon shone
bright above, her young voice was soft but clear.
"Thank you, Oak Tree, she whispered.
"Thank you for giving me courage."
"Now Sister Eagle," said the Oak Tree,
"Soar as high as your wings can take you."

And his leaves shimmered silver in the moonlight.

The End

Stories have the power to heal. As a primary school teacher, I often found opportunities to nourish the inner life of a child by creating a story. *The Eagle Flew* is one of those; written and told for a child in need of encouragement to overcome a host of fears, trust her gifts, find her voice and spread her wings to fly. It's a story best suited for ages 4-9.

Beautiful and imaginative pictures also nourish the soul. The illustrator of the book, Aisha Wiig, was one of my students 30 years ago, who fortunately stayed in contact with me. As early as third grade, her artistry shimmered off the page. When she agreed to work with me, it was one of those rare, full-circle blessings that seemed to drop from the sky.